ON THE HARDWOOD

DETROIT PISTONS

J.M. SKOGEN

On the Hardwood: Detroit Pistons

MVP Books
2255 Calle Clara
La Jolla, CA 92037

MVP Books is an imprint of Scobre Educational, a division of Book Buddy Digital Media, Inc.,
42982 Osgood Road, Fremont, CA 94539

MVP Books publications may be purchased for educational, business, or sales promotional use.

Cover and layout design by Jana Ramsay
Copyedited by Susan Sylvia
Photos by Getty Images

ISBN: 978-1-61570-910-6 (Library Binding)
ISBN: 978-1-61570-909-0 (Soft Cover)

TABLE OF CONTENTS

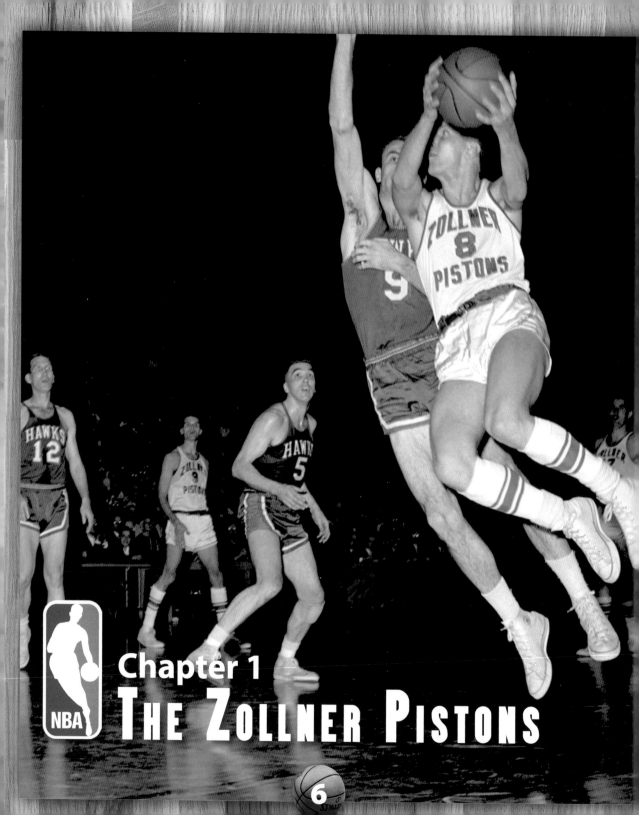

Chapter 1
THE ZOLLNER PISTONS

Over the years, the Detroit Pistons have developed a reputation for being tough, determined "Bad Boys" who will get the job done. They are three-time NBA Champions, with a history of gritty, nail-biting games, and stunning victories. The Pistons also stand among the oldest NBA franchises in the league. Indeed, they were one of the original 17 NBA teams when the league was founded in 1949.

Unlike many other NBA teams, the Detroit Pistons are not represented by an animal (like the Chicago Bulls, and the Memphis Grizzlies). Nor are they a force of nature

(like the Oklahoma City Thunder, or the Miami Heat). Their name is also not a type of person (the Portland Trail Blazers, and the Washington Wizards, for example). A "piston" is a man-made invention, and a key part of an internal combustion engine. Without a piston, most cars simply

1989 WORLD CHAMPIONS

1990 WORLD CHAMPIONS

PISTONS 2004 WORLD CHAMPIONS

The Pistons' three championship banners hang proudly in Detroit's Palace.

7

A car factory in Detroit, Michigan.

DO NOT CROSS

would not run. Detroit, Michigan, the home of the Pistons, is known as the Automotive Capital of the World, or more simply as Motor City. Nestled on the border of Canada, surrounded by the Great Lakes, Detroit is the one of the biggest producers of cars in the country. Given how perfectly the Pistons' name matches their current home, it would surprise many people to learn that the Pistons were not originally from the Motor City.

The Pistons' first home was actually Fort Wayne, Indiana—a much smaller city than bustling Detroit. A man named Fred Zollner ran a business in Fort Wayne: a foundry that produced—you guessed it—pistons. The Pistons began, not as an NBA team, but as a team in the National Basketball

League (NBL) in 1941. Zollner named his team after the vital engine part that his company manufactured. They were the Fort Wayne Zollner Pistons. Their team logo was a metallic man made entirely out of pistons, dribbling a basketball. On his chest, was the letter "Z" for Zollner. The Zollner Pistons started out playing in a local high school gym—a venue that made for some very exciting games due to its small size. Fans were often literally in the middle of the action.

Zollner's team had some great accomplishments during their eight years in the NBL.

From 1942 to 1945, the Zollner Pistons advanced to the NBL Finals every season. They even won NBL Championships in 1944 and 1945. This was during the final years of World War II—a time of turmoil, heartache, and uncertainty. The town of Fort Wayne was so proud to watch

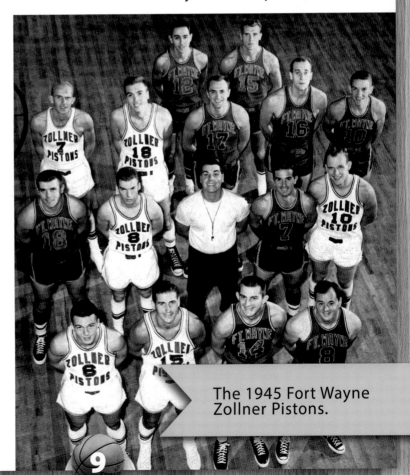

The 1945 Fort Wayne Zollner Pistons.

their team (wearing patriotic red, white and blue team colors) become champions.

In 1949, the NBL merged with the Basketball Association of America (BAA) to form the National Basketball Association (NBA). The Fort Wayne Zollner Pistons decided that they needed a shorter name for their new league. They eventually cut "Zollner" completely, and just went by "Fort Wayne Pistons." Owner Fred Zollner, however, remained a vital part of the team, and was instrumental to the early success of the NBA. In fact, Zollner was one of the key people responsible for the BAA / NBL merger. In 1949, Zollner invited leaders of the NBL and BAA over to his house. It was at this meeting that they agreed to merge the two leagues to form the NBA. Though Zollner passed away in 1982 at the age of 81, the world of basketball continued to honor

Fort Wayne is now home to the Mad Ants, a team in the NBA Development League.

his memory. In 1999, Fred Zollner was inducted into the Basketball Hall of Fame.

Though they did not immediately reach the same heights in the NBA as they did in the NBL, the Pistons were playoff contenders every single season from 1950 to 1957. Though the Pistons had a loyal fan base in Fort Wayne, Zollner decided that his team would fair better in a bigger city. The Pistons adored their fans, but there wasn't always enough support from the city of Fort Wayne. For example, when the Pistons advanced to the NBA Finals in 1955, the Fort Wayne Memorial Coliseum

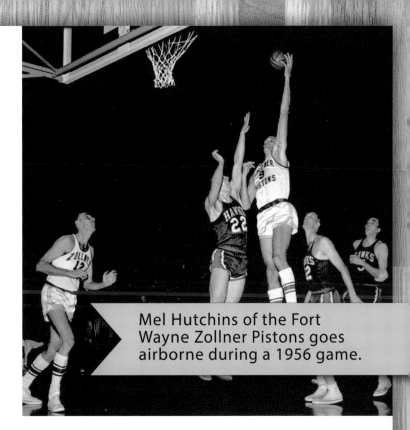

Mel Hutchins of the Fort Wayne Zollner Pistons goes airborne during a 1956 game.

was already booked for a national bowling tournament. The Pistons were not even able to play their home games in Fort Wayne, and were forced to relocate to Indianapolis for the NBA Finals.

Detroit's Hoops History
In 1946-47, two basketball teams played in Detroit: the Detroit Falcons and the Detroit Gems. The Gems later became the L.A. Lakers.

In 1957, the Pistons moved to Detroit—a location that Zollner thought would be big enough to support his franchise. Since Detroit's bread and butter was the auto manufacturing industry, Zollner thought that the "Pistons" was still the perfect name for his team. They became simply the Detroit Pistons.

Detroit was supposed to be the place where the Pistons finally had room to grow, and match—or even exceed—their early NBL potential. Over the next few decades, they did have some good seasons, and some spectacular players. For example, in the 1957-58 season, future Hall-of-Famer George Yardley was the first NBA player in the league's history to score 2,000 points in a single season. However, the 1960s and 1970s proved to be a pretty long dry spell for the Pistons. Though they advanced to the playoffs several times, they were never really championship contenders. Between 1957 and 1980, they

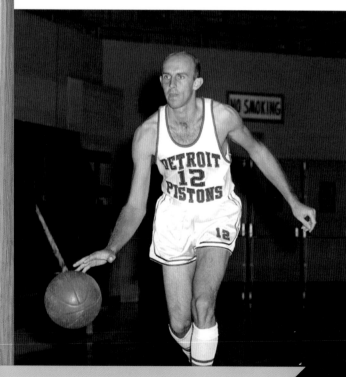

George Yardley was one of the Detroit Pistons' first stars.

only had three winning seasons.

By 1979-80, the Pistons were at the bottom of the NBA heap. Their regular season record was a dismal 16-66. This was a franchise worst, and the worst record in the league that season. The following season wasn't much better. The Pistons tallied a 21-61 record, earning them the 2nd pick in the NBA Draft. Years later, Pistons fans would be grateful for that horrible season, and their lucky draft pick. After decades of mediocrity, and years of failure, they heard the sweetest words possible on that wonderful 1981 draft day: "Detroit picks six-foot one, 180 pound, Isiah Thomas."

Isiah Thomas drives past Gerald Henderson of the Celtics during his first season with the Pistons.

As Isiah Thomas took the stage at the 1981 NBA Draft and shook the announcer's hand, a huge grin lit up his face. Thomas was clean cut, and looked natural in a suit and tie. Though he was just starting his professional basketball career, he also had ambitions to continue his education, and eventually become a lawyer. Thomas looked like someone you would want to be friends with—he was always smiling.

However, Isiah Thomas hadn't always had so much to smile about. He grew up in a very poor family, and was the youngest of nine children. *Sports Illustrated* reported how there was never enough food, and sometimes "Isiah's mother, Mary, whom he describes as 'the greatest woman in the world,' would take food from the cafeteria where she worked." Though Thomas excelled at basketball, he knew that things like health and athleticism could be fleeting. He wanted something concrete that he could always fall back on—like an education. In fact, Thomas completed his degree from the Indiana University while playing for the Pistons, and eventually

Isiah Thomas: happy to be a Piston.

earned a Masters of Education in 2013.

Compared to many basketball greats, Isiah Thomas was small—he was only 6'2". But his opponents soon learned to never underestimate his easy grin

Bill Laimbeer fights for a rebound against the Washington Bullets.

and short stature. While still a sophomore at the University of Indiana, Thomas led the Hoosiers to the 1981 NCAA Championship. Thomas then rode that victory straight to the NBA—electing to participate in the draft at the end of the 1980-81 season. Once in a Pistons uniform, opposing teams started calling Thomas the "Smiling Assassin" for his big grin and killer moves on the court.

With Thomas already heating up the hardwood, a series of in-season trades in 1982 further strengthened the Pistons' roster. Bill Laimbeer, who came to Detroit from the Cleveland Cavaliers, proved to be one of the most skilled centers in the NBA. Laimbeer led the Pistons in rebounds, had a great outside shot, and—teamed up with Thomas— had an almost unstoppable pick-and-roll. Another acquisition was Vinnie "the Microwave" Johnson. Johnson got his nickname because he could come off the bench and "heat up fast."

Indeed, these players all contributed to a nearly 180-degree turnaround for the Detroit Pistons, as they hauled themselves up from 21-61, to a more respectable 39-43 regular season record. However, the Pistons' General Manager, Jack McCloskey, (or "Trader Jack" as he came to be known, for all of his successful trades) was not satisfied with "respectable." He wanted to see Detroit dominate in the postseason, and become champions. For this to happen, McCloskey

decided that he needed a new coach to lead the improving team.

Trader Jack had one person in mind—his old friend Chuck Daly. Daly had risen through the ranks: coaching in high school, college, then joined the NBA as an assistant coach for the 76ers. Eventually, he was hired as the head coach of the Cleveland Cavaliers during the 1981-82 season. Though Daly was a veteran with many coaching honors already under his belt, he did not find success in Cleveland. The Cavaliers had a record of 4-14 when he arrived in

From the Playbook

The pick-and-roll is a play where an offensive player sets a screen, or a "pick," so the teammate with the ball can get around a defensive player. The screening player then "rolls" away, and is open for a pass. This play is very popular.

Coach Daly chats with Isiah Thomas during a game in 1985.

bother McCloskey: "I know the record wasn't good in Cleveland, but I knew he could coach," McCloskey said. "(Cleveland) didn't have anything. When I saw him in his college days, I knew he was a good motivator. I knew he had good communication skills."

After Chuck Daly arrived in Detroit, the Pistons gave their new coach the nickname "Daddy Rich" for his perfect hair, and great sense of style. Daly was not only one of the best dressed coaches in the league, he also brought out the best in his players. By 1983-84, the Pistons were not just tallying an "average" or "respectable" record—they were playoff contenders every year.

December of 1981, and they had a dreary 13-46 record when he was replaced in February 1982.

McCloskey saw Chuck Daly's departure from Cleveland as a huge opportunity for the Pistons. Trader Jack had previously tried to lure Coach Daly to Detroit several years earlier, when Daly was still an assistant coach for the 76ers. And Daly's record in Cleveland didn't

While other teams had celebrities like Michael Jordan,

Magic Johnson, and Larry Bird, the Pistons did not really have one huge star. Sure, Isiah Thomas was the Pistons' team leader, and he would eventually be selected as an All-Star every year from 1982 to 1993. But for all of his success, Thomas did not have the same level of basketball fame as some of the other NBA celebrities. Coach Daly described his scrappy team: "if we and the Lakers lined up next to each other five-on-five, position-by-position, we come out on the short end. They're studs—they make us look like a mongrel team." The Pistons needed something more than star-quality, and a one-man offensive powerhouse like Jordan. They needed an unbeatable, crushing defense.

Suit Up

Coach Daly was known for wearing a signature blue suit. In an interview, Daly once claimed to own 200 suits!

During the mid 1980s, the Detroit Pistons developed a tough-as-nails defensive strategy that became famous for one main fact— no one wanted to play against them. Detroit fought hard for every point, and developed a reputation for playing "overly aggressive." Their take-no-prisoners attitude on the court earned the Pistons the nickname: the Motor City "Bad Boys." Rather than shy away from this somewhat negative name, Detroit embraced it. They even wore black practice jerseys that read "Bad Boys," complete with the logo of a skull and crossbones over a basketball— like a pirate flag.

Dennis Rodman flies up to grab a reboud during a 1987 game against Houston.

him. They love to hate him. It's a love-hate relationship. Tell you the truth, if I didn't know Bill, I wouldn't like him either."

Another stand-out "Bad Boy" was Dennis Rodman. Rodman came to the Pistons in the 1986 NBA Draft, and he became a key part of Detroit's militant defense. He would doggedly pursue every rebound, and fearlessly throw his body into the middle of any scrap for the ball. The NBA eventually honored Rodman with back-to-back Defensive Player of the Year awards for the 1989-90 and 1990-91 seasons.

Of these "Bad Boys," Bill Laimbeer was the baddest of them all. He became famous for his aggressiveness on the court. Other teams hated to play against him. In fact, some of his nicknames included "His Heiness," and "The Prince of Darkness." Isiah Thomas once said of Lambeer: "I wouldn't say fans hate

Pistons fans loved their team's new "Bad Boy" persona. Detroit was a city built on hard labor and motor oil. In the center of the industrial "Rust Belt" of America,

Getting Defensive
During his NBA career, Dennis Rodman was selected for the All-Defensive first team seven times.

Motor City respected hard work and determination. They were proud to see their team standing up to the best teams in the NBA, and thrilled that they were actually winning.

In 1987-88, the Pistons advanced to the NBA Finals for the first time since 1954—and the first time since the team moved to Detroit. They were firing on all cylinders—scorching up the court against the Los Angeles Lakers. The series went to seven knock-down, drag-out games—and the whole city of Detroit was on the edge of its seat. Was this the year that their team finally took home an NBA Championship?

Unfortunately, the Lakers, with stars like Kareem Abdul-

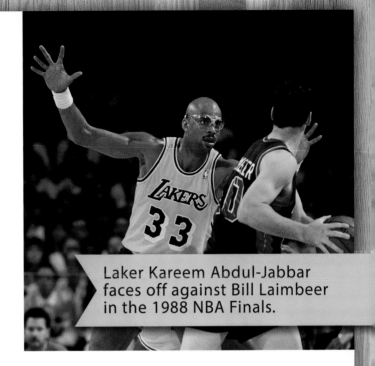

Laker Kareem Abdul-Jabbar faces off against Bill Laimbeer in the 1988 NBA Finals.

Jabbar, Magic Johnson, and James Worthy, proved to be too much for the Pistons, and they lost Game 7. However, the whole season had been a kind of victory, because the country now realized that the Detroit Pistons could challenge the best that the NBA had to offer. Detroit, and the rest of the basketball world, were excited to see what the next few years would bring.

The 1989 NBA Finals

Chapter 3
A New Dynasty

The 1980s was a fantastic decade to be in the NBA—if you happened to play for the Boston Celtics or the Los Angeles Lakers. From 1980 to 1988, the Lakers took home five NBA Championships, and the Celtics ran away with three. So, when the Detroit Pistons started to make some noise during the 1988-89 season, they weren't just trying to win their first NBA Championship—they were aiming to topple the ruling East and West Coast NBA dynasties.

Adrian Dantley drives to the basket in a 1987 game against the L.A. Lakers.

The 1987-88 season, ending in a battle against the Lakers in the NBA Finals, had proven that Detroit was one of the elite teams in basketball. However, the Pistons didn't want to be one of many—they wanted to be number one. In the middle of the next season, Detroit made a startling trade to try to strengthen their already stellar team. They traded Adrian Dantley, and a future #1 draft pick, to the Dallas Mavericks for star forward Mark Aguirre. This trade was highly criticized. Adrian Dantley was a strong player, and many fans did not want the Pistons to make serious roster changes when they had come so far in the previous season. But Trader Jack, and other members of the Pistons' management, thought that there was still room to improve and grow. They hoped that, with a few minor adjustments, the Pistons would finally go that extra mile.

Mark Aguirre—who had been the #1 pick in the 1981 Draft, just ahead of Isiah Thomas—was also Thomas's childhood friend. Though the Pistons had an unmatched defensive game, Aguirre added quick-paced offense to the team. With his help, the Pistons were soon dominating all aspects of the game.

The Pistons had another huge change at the start of the 1988-89 season. For years they had been playing in the Pontiac Silverdome—an 80,000 seat, monster of a building, when most NBA arenas held closer to 20,000 fans. The Silverdome was really meant for a different kind of sporting event, like football. In fact, even in the NFL, the Silverdome was one of the

Mark Aguirre was the final piece on the Pistons' 1989 championship roster.

largest venues. Going to a game at the Silverdome felt like watching basketball in a huge cave. With much joy, the Pistons finally moved into an arena that was actually intended for basketball games. The Palace of Auburn Hills, often just called "The Palace," could hold a cozier 21,454 fans, and was closer to where most of the Pistons fans actually lived. Fans flocked to fill their new arena. The Palace boasted sell-out attendance from its opening on November 5th, 1988, until December of 1993—tallying 245 consecutive games.

Detroit now had the challenge of bringing home a crown to their new Palace. They started

off the 1988-89 season with engines roaring. The Pistons earned the best regular season record in the NBA: 63-19. The "Bad Boys" continued to prove their dominance with a no-contest victory over the East Coast Dynasty—they beat the Boston Celtics 4-0 in the first round of the

Detroit's new "Palace."

25

postseason. Then, they flattened the Milwaukee Bucks 4-0 in the Eastern Conference Semifinals. It was starting to look like nothing could possibly get in their way.

However, to reach the NBA Finals, the Pistons first had to get past the Chicago Bulls. More specifically, they had to beat Michael Jordan. To combat Chicago, Coach Chuck Daly had come up with a specific strategy for dealing with Jordan. This strategy came to be known as the "Jordan Rules." According to *Sports Illustrated*: "There were three tenets to the Detroit defense: Never give Jordan an easy shot; try to confuse him with varied defensive looks; and be very physical with him." Many people thought that 1988-89 would be Michael Jordan's season, and he would finally bring the Chicago Bulls a title. However, even though Jordan played

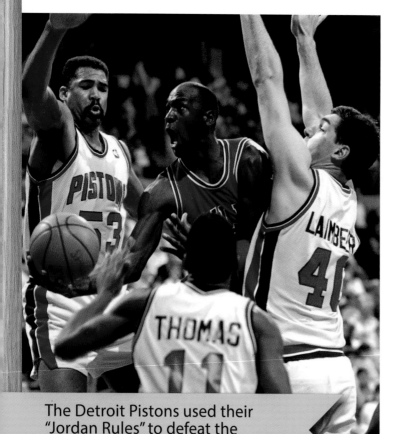

The Detroit Pistons used their "Jordan Rules" to defeat the Chicago Bulls in the 1989 playoffs.

with his usual domination on the court—he averaged 34 points and seven assists per game during the playoff series—the Bad Boys from Detroit and their "Jordan Rules" still overwhelmed him.

At the end of the 4-2 series, it was the Pistons who advanced to the NBA Finals. For the second season in a row, Detroit had a real chance at greatness.

The 1989 NBA Finals looked a lot like the 1988 NBA Finals as the Detroit Pistons once again faced off against the L.A. Lakers. People even took to calling it "The Sequel." Detroit, however, was convinced that their rematch would have a very different ending.

The Pistons handily won the first game at home. When they returned to the Palace for Game 2, Detroit was eager to notch another win in the series. The Pistons played well—Joe Dumars scored an incredible 24 points in the first half of the game. However, for all of Detroit's efforts, the Lakers rallied. At half-time, the Pistons trailed 62-56. "The Sequel" was beginning to look like a true repeat of last season's NBA Finals, where the Pistons and the Lakers traded victories all the way to Game 7.

In the third quarter, with the game tied at 75, Lakers' star, Magic Johnson, pulled a hamstring. As he hobbled off the court in

Winning Smile

After Isiah Thomas took home the 1990 Finals MVP award, he smiled and said "You can say what you want about me, but you can't say that I'm not a winner."

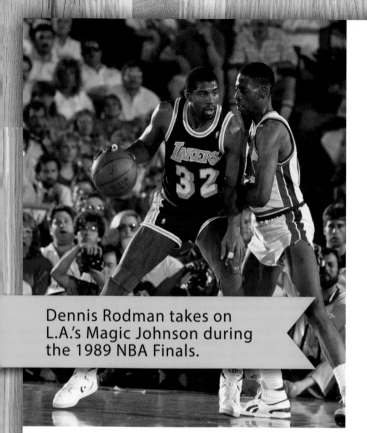

Dennis Rodman takes on L.A.'s Magic Johnson during the 1989 NBA Finals.

gear in the fourth quarter.

Detroit did not disappoint. The Pistons battled for every rebound and fought for each point. Dennis Rodman, who had earlier that day been to the hospital with a back injury, was back on the floor, throwing himself into the action, drawing offensive fouls. Detroit managed to score eight points in the first four minutes of the fourth quarter, before the Lakers even scored one.

Near the end of the fourth quarter, the Pistons led 106-104. When the Lakers' James Worthy drew a foul with only two seconds left on the clock, the Lakers had a final chance to tie up the score, and push the game into overtime.

terrible pain, the audience wondered if losing Johnson would be the final straw for L.A. The Lakers, however, only seemed more motivated by their star's injury, and racked up a 15-6 point run. L.A. led by eight at the end of the third quarter. If the Pistons were going to take Game 2, they had to find a new

Worthy lined up, got ready. Then—clang. The first shot bounced off the rim. He made the second shot, but it was of no use—Detroit was clinging to a one point lead. Then, with one second left, Isiah Thomas was fouled. Thomas made both shots, and it was over. The Pistons had won the first two games in the Palace.

Joe Dumars and Isiah Thomas ride proud in the 1989 Detroit Pistons Victory Parade.

After this nail-biting Game 2 win, the Pistons truly could not be stopped. They closed the 1989 NBA Finals with a 4-0 series victory against the Lakers. Detroit had finally done it. For the first time in their 40 year history, they were NBA Champions. When the Pistons followed up their 1989 victory with another NBA title in 1990, Motor City was beyond thrilled. The Bad Boys were not only at the top of their game, but they were the new ruling dynasty in the NBA.

Making History

The L.A. Lakers swept three teams before they reached the NBA Finals, only to be swept by the Pistons. This was the first time that a team with a perfect playoffs record was swept in the finals.

Chapter 4
RETURN TO GLORY

After the Pistons captured the NBA title two years in a row, fans enthusiastically wondered how long Detroit would rule the NBA. Unfortunately, the Chicago Bulls ousted the Pistons in the 1991 Eastern Conference Finals, and went on to win the crown for themselves. For the next decade, the Bulls, led by Michael Jordan, dominated in the postseason—winning six NBA championships, and firmly declaring themselves the new dynasty.

Detroit—and almost every team that was not Chicago—had several discouraging years waiting for Michael Jordan's team to finally come back to earth after rising so high.

Roster changes on the Pistons' team, including the retirement of Isiah Thomas and Bill Laimbeer in 1994, meant that Detroit had some rebuilding seasons ahead. For about 10 years, Detroit was no longer part of the ruling class in the NBA. They occasionally visited the postseason, but usually made swift first round exits.

During one of his final games as a Piston, Isiah Thomas drives past Utah Jazz's John Stockton.

The Pistons retired Joe Dumars' number on March 10th, 2000.

In 1999, one of the Pistons' last remaining players from the Bad Boys era, Joe Dumars, retired from playing basketball, but his career was far from over. He stayed in Detroit, and became the Pistons' President of Basketball Operations. Dumars—

Pistons for Sale?

In 1996, while still a Piston, Joe Dumars became majority owner and CEO of an emerging automotive parts supplier called Detroit Technologies

who had been awarded NBA Finals MVP in 1989—had played his entire professional career in Motor City. He was determined that, under his watch, the Pistons would once again rise to glory. Dumars got to work—making roster and coaching changes to bolster Detroit's chemistry and talent on the court. In doing so, Dumars did not simply seek out established NBA stars. He looked for players with great potential, even those whose careers had stalled on other NBA teams. In 2002, Dumars added two players who would become the new core of the Pistons: free agent Chauncey Billups, and former Washington Wizard Richard "Rip" Hamilton.

When Billups put on the

Pistons' jersey, he was already an experienced player—he had played in the NBA for five years. In those five years, however, Billups had been on five different teams, including the Boston Celtics, Denver Nuggets, and Minnesota Timberwolves. It wasn't until a breakout 2001-02 season with the Timberwolves that Billups really showed the NBA world that he was a future star. With a teammate injured

Team Legacy
In 2004, Chauncey Billups was the first point guard to win the NBA Finals MVP award since Isiah Thomas in 1990.

going into the postseason, Billups filled in as starting point guard. He scored an incredible 22 points per game in the first round of the playoffs before the Timberwolves lost to Dallas. Dumars was thrilled to add Billups to his rebuilding team once he became a free-agent. Finally

Chauncey Billups drives to the basket against the Golden State Warriors during a 2003 game.

able to stay in one place, instead of being passed around from team to team, Billups had a real chance to become a team leader.

Shooting guard Richard "Rip" Hamilton, on the other hand, had been with the Washington Wizards since the 1999 NBA Draft, when he was the 7th overall pick. Though Hamilton had a lot of potential, the Washington Wizards were not a winning team in the late 1990s and early 2000s. They had not been to the playoffs since 1997. During the 2001-02 season, NBA great (and former Pistons rival) Michael Jordan joined the Wizards' roster, where he became a mentor to Hamilton. That season, Hamilton tallied a solid 20 points per game, and was beginning to get some attention from the NBA world. When the Pistons traded their top scorer, Jerry Stackhouse, to the Wizards in 2002 for Hamilton and two other players, fans hoped that the gamble would pay off.

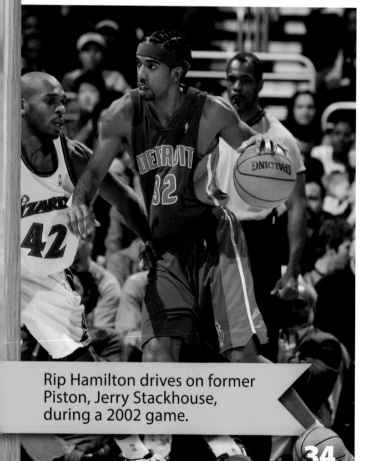

Rip Hamilton drives on former Piston, Jerry Stackhouse, during a 2002 game.

With Billups and Hamilton forming a solid backcourt, the Pistons started to heat up almost immediately. In 2002-03, Detroit advanced to the Eastern Conference Finals for the first time since 1991. Though the New Jersey Nets took the series, the Pistons knew that they were on the right track.

Going into the 2003-04 season, the Pistons were once again at the top of their game. However, for all of their talent, the Pistons were different than most of the elite NBA teams in one noticeable way: they did not have a superstar on their team. Sure, Billups and Hamilton were both having great seasons, but neither

one was really a huge figure in the NBA world. What they *did* have was unmatched teamwork on the court. While the Pistons' last championship players were famous for being "Bad Boys," the 2003-04 team was known

Chauncey Billups and Rip Hamilton: the backcourt core of the 2003-04 Pistons.

"Big Ben" Wallace slams it home during the 2004 All-Star game at Staples Center.

for their ability to work together to form a staggering defense and a sharp-shooting offense. No one tried to steal the spotlight, and everyone worked toward a common goal: victory.

Several other players, along with Billups and Hamilton, helped form the unforgettable 2004 Pistons team. There was 6' 9", 240-pound forward-center Ben Wallace, who won the NBA Defensive Player of the Year Award four times between 2001 and 2006. He was known as "The Body" and "Big Ben," for his huge size and power on the court. When he scored at home, the Pistons would often play a loud clock chime—a reference to the real Big Ben, a famous clock-tower in London.

Then there was the other Wallace—Rasheed Wallace. Rasheed

was a dynamo of a forward-center, who arrived in a trade from the Atlanta Hawks in the middle of the 2003-04 season. Dumars had been looking to add someone just like Rasheed to their roster: a big man who could tackle both offense and defense, with lots of energy to spare. They hoped that Rasheed would be the new element that they needed to push their already fantastic team to the next level.

Rasheed Wallace goes for a slam dunk during Game 3 of the 2004 NBA Finals.

Another key player on the 2003-04 roster was Tayshaun Prince. Prince had been drafted by Detroit in 2002, but didn't really come into his own until the 2003 playoffs—where he actually scored more points in the postseason than he did in the regular season. This was an NBA first. Under new head coach Larry Brown, Prince was elevated from a backup player to starting small forward for the 2003-04 season.

Coach Brown, who joined the Pistons in 2003, was a good fit for this team of travelers. Like many of the players, Coach Brown had been all around the country during his coaching career. Since 1988, Brown had coached the San Antonio Spurs, Los Angeles Clippers, Indiana Pacers, and Philidelphia 76ers before landing in Detroit. He knew how to coach many different personalities and worked hard to bring out each player's individual strengths. Brown was also no stranger to the playoffs. Coach Brown has tallied the fourth most wins in NBA playoffs history.

With their new coach, and solid roster, the Pistons raced through the 2004 playoffs. They advanced to the NBA Finals for the first time in 14 years. Detroit was thrilled, but many critics thought that this was the end of the road for the scrappy team from Motor City. They would once again face off against the Los Angeles Lakers, who were overwhelming favorites to win the series. The Lakers came armed with veterans like Karl Malone and Gary Payton, and superstars like Shaquille O'Neal and Kobe Bryant. These were royal names in the basketball world, while the Pistons were just a "group of guys."

New Pistons Coach Larry Brown and Joe Dumars smile during a 2003 press conference.

Ultimately, the series went to five games. In four of those five games, the Pistons beat the Lakers so thoroughly, that the series became known as the "five game sweep." Even though the Pistons did not have celebrities with big names, in the end, they didn't need

them. Detroit had a work-ethic that was unparallelled in the NBA at that time. The Pistons didn't need one big star. They were all champions.

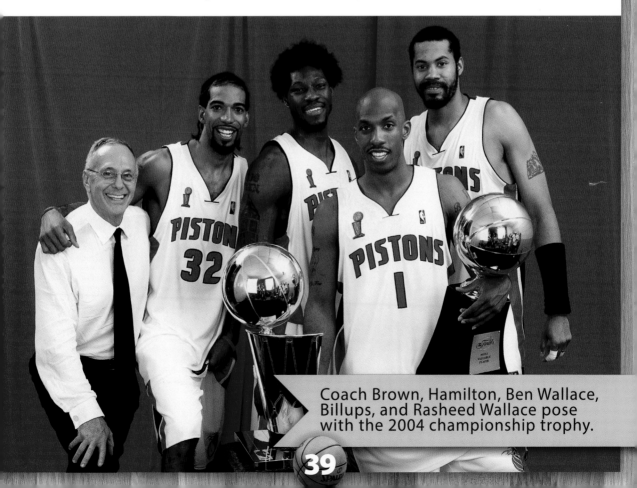

Coach Brown, Hamilton, Ben Wallace, Billups, and Rasheed Wallace pose with the 2004 championship trophy.

Chapter 5

BUILDING THE FUTURE

After taking home their third NBA Championship title in 2004, it looked like Motor City's reign might last for another year. When the Pistons advanced to the NBA Finals again in 2005, Detroit fans were beyond excited—clamoring for another back-to-back title victory. Unfortunately, the San Antonio Spurs took home the title—one of three NBA Championships that the Spurs won from 2003 to 2007. However, the Pistons were still championship contenders, and visited the Eastern Conference Finals each year from 2006 to 2008.

The 2007-08 season—when they fought, and lost, the Eastern Conference Finals to the Boston Celtics—would prove to be the end of an era for the Pistons. Looking to build on a young, exciting roster, the Pistons traded Chauncey Billups, along with a few other players, to the Denver Nuggets for Allen Iverson. Iverson was a superstar who was supposed to assist the roster in tandem with up-and-coming point guard Rodney Stuckey.

Many fans were saddened by Billups' departure. Over the

Rodney Stuckey and Allen Iverson take the court before a 2009 game in Memphis.

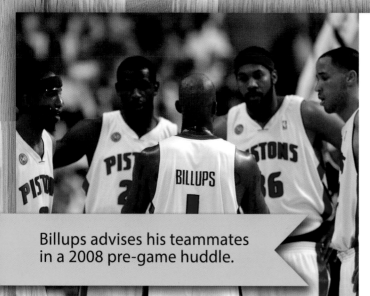

Billups advises his teammates in a 2008 pre-game huddle.

roster was not set in stone, and a team must grow and change so it can improve over time. It was simply hard to see such a successful period of Pistons' history come to an end.

As with most teams in a rebuilding stage, the new Pistons team struggled to find its footing. Also, Iverson, who had constant back injuries, didn't live up to expectations as a Piston. He was deactivated near the end of the 2008-09 season, leaving the Pistons without a key player on their roster.

years, Billups had become the face of the Pistons. He was viewed as the calm, stable glue that held the many outgoing personalities on the team together, and enabled their exceptional teamwork. Fans wondered if this roster change would rock the boat a little too much. However, even the most skeptical critics recognized that a

The Pistons made the playoffs in 2009, but lost in the first round. Then, to Detroit's disappointment, the Pistons began missing the postseason entirely

Shoes for Sale

In 2009, Rodney Stuckey sold his size 18 shoes in an online auction to raise money for charity. They sold for $150.

Owner Bill Davidson uses spray paint to mark off the 41st straight sell-out game during the 2004-05 season.

starting in 2009-10. During this dark time, the Pistons experienced an even bigger loss. Their owner, Bill Davidson, died in 2009 at the age of 86. In their long history, the Pistons had only had two owners—Fred Zollner from their Fort Wayne days, and then Davidson, who had bought the Pistons from Zollner in 1974. Davidson had been a kind, supportive presence over the years—doing everything he could to help the Pistons prosper.

For example, when Detroit built The Palace in 1988, it was Davidson who footed the entire bill for the new arena. Though Davidson had long said that the Pistons' would remain in his family after his death, there was still a lot of uncertainly, along with grief, after he passed away.

Eventually, in 2011, Bill Davidson's wife sold the Pistons to Tom Gores, a self-made billionaire who ranked #153 on *Forbes Magazine's* list of

Triple Threat

While in high school, Tom Gores was a star basketball, football, and baseball player.

the top 400 richest Americans. Tom Gores was not a stranger to Detroit. He had grown up in the small town of Genesee, Michigan, and went to college at Michigan State. Always an avid sports fan, Gores was very competitive in high school. Even while running his private equity firm, Platinum Equity, Gores values time with his three children and is an active and avid coach of youth soccer and basketball. Tom Gores not only had a huge financial stake in seeing the Pistons succeed, but had a great deal of pride in his team, and state.

Though Detroit was still firmly in a rebuilding stage for the first few years of Gores' ownership, by the end of the 2012-13 season, there was a lot to be optimistic about. After acquiring free agent Josh Smith in July 2013, the Pistons suddenly had three big men who could bring the franchise back to the top.

Josh Smith, who came to the Pistons from the Atlanta

New Pistons owner Tom Gores (left) poses with Ethan Davidson (former owner Bill Davidson's son).

44

Hawks, was a forceful, and versatile player. At 6' 9", Smith could play small or power forward. In 2010, he was also the youngest player to ever record 1,000 blocks. Smith was quite young to be a nine-year NBA veteran—only 27 years old. This was because he entered the draft right after high school, and never looked back. Smith, or "J-Smoove" as he is often called, played at an elite level from an early age. In high school, Smith took the court with future NBA players like Rajon Rondo and Dwight Howard. During his senior year, Rivals.com ranked Smith as the best small forward, and third best overall player in the country. In a press release, Joe Dumars summed up the talent that the Pistons had gained by signing

Before joining the Pistons, Josh Smith tore up the hardwood for the Hawks.

Smith: "We looked at all of the free agents out there that could come in and help elevate us, elevate our talent level, elevate our ability to have chances to win games, and Josh was that guy for us. It's a good

Top of the Class

In addition to being one of the best high school basketball players in the country, Josh Smith also earned the best grades in his high school class in 2003-04.

Happy fans line up for Drummond's autograph at a 2013 Pistons event.

Drummond was just 19 years old when he began his professional career. During his rookie season, Drummond only played an average of 20 minutes per game, but he scored an impressive 7.9 points per game. In May of 2013, 6'10", 270-pound Drummond was selected to the NBA All-Rookie second team—confirming Detroit's belief that, in Drummond, they had found a future star.

day for us.'"

The two other players who formed the big-man core of the team were Andre Drummond and Greg Monroe—both young, powerful players. Drummond arrived in Detroit as the 9th overall pick in the 2012 NBA Draft. Having chosen to enter the NBA Draft after his freshman year of college,

Greg Monroe, the Pistons' top scorer, had joined the Pistons in the 2010 NBA Draft. Being drafted by a team that was not at the top of the NBA heap did not bother Monroe. Indeed, he had a history of weathering adversity, and working to make things better. When he was just 15 years old, in New

Orleans, Monroe and his family had to flee from Hurricane Katrina. When they returned, rather than despair over their destroyed house, and devastated neighborhood, Monroe tried to set things right. He was there with a hammer to help fix up his own house. Rebuilding a franchise is not at all on the same level as recovering from a natural disaster. However, Monroe was more than ready to bring his determination, and great work ethic, to help Detroit return to brighter days.

At the end of the 2012-13 season, Detroit received some more exciting news: Chauncey Billups had re-signed with the Pistons for two years. It looked like Billups would be able to retire a Piston. Players like Stuckey, who had played with Billups before he was traded, were thrilled to have a legend returning to Motor City. In addition to Billups, another 2004 Champion, Rasheed Wallace,

Greg Monroe scores against the Knicks' Jason Kidd and Carmelo Anthony in a 2013 game.

was also coming back to Detroit. Rasheed, however, would not be playing, but would be serving as assistant coach to the Pistons.

Another promising roster change came in July 2013. The Pistons traded Brandon Knight, and two other players, to the Milwaukee Bucks for point guard Brandon Jennings. Jennings will bring his 17 points per game average, and a mountain of potential, to Detroit, where he will join Monroe, Drummond, Stuckey, and Smith as a potential starter.

Over the years, the Detroit Pistons have proven that they have a lot in common with their Motor City home. They know how to work hard, and build great things. With a young, exciting roster, and guidance from returning champions like Chauncey Billups, there is no limit to the Pistons' potential in the coming years. One day soon, the Pistons are sure to find the right gear, and will rejoin the NBA elite in the race for a championship.

Chauncey Billups: a Piston again.